So Beautiful As You

An Illuminative Journey of Heart Warming Floral Creations

An Illuminative Journey of Heart Warming Floral Creations

Mother Ahavah
DR. ANN MARIE NIELSEN

the NAMELESS
SPEAKS
PUBLICATIONS

So Beautiful As You:

An Illuminative Journey of Heart Warming Floral Creations

Floral Creations, Contemplative Titles, Photographs, Floral Borders,
Cover Art and Cover design by Dr. Ann Marie Nielsen, Mother Ahavah

Copyright © 2018 by Dr. Ann Marie Nielsen, Mother Ahavah

All rights reserved.
No part of this book may be reproduced or transmitted in any form without the express permission in writing from the publisher, except by a reviewer who may quote brief passages for review purposes.

FIRST EDITION 2018   ISBN-13: 978-0-9975228-8-4   ISBN-10: 0-9975228-8-7

Published by The Nameless Speaks Publications, Florida USA

www.motherahavah.com

Available worldwide from Amazon and other online and traditional book sellers

Contents

Prelude, and Letter to the Reader..... 9

Love Loves For No Reason..... 17

Paradise, Be the Beauty Essence of the Changeless-Afresh Pure Land Inside ... Everywhere..... 19

Fall In Love With Love Knowing Itself..... 21

Hallelujah Peace, Celestial Sovereign Awareness..... 23

Authentic Genius, Cradles Incandescent Innocence In Bold Realness..... 25

I Am The Silence Of Love's Tender Exalting Crescendo..... 27

Soft Is True..... 29

The Prolific Heart, The Garden of Spontaneous Joy-Nurture At Home..... 31

I Am Here For Life..... 33

Simple Bald Vulnerability, Endures In Eternal Clean Welcome..... 35

Tangible White Knowing, Seamless Holy Intimacy Knowing Itself, Everyone Smiles Now..... 37

Before Time Ivory white Silence Birthed my Essence As Original Stillness..... 39

Bless Each Moment See Gentle Peace Dawn..... 41

Delicate Goodness Power On-the-Spot..... 43

Cocoon the Potent Focus..... 45

Compassion is the Priestess of the Prolific Industriousness..... 47

Delicate Freedom Fresh to Bond in Each Moment 49

Jubilant in Unified Non Attachment 51

Instantaneity, Tomorrow's Promise Happens Now 53

Joy Is Opening to Be Deeply Touched 55

Vulnerability Is Strength When We Rest As the Sheen of Acceptance 57

Love Finds Safe Passageway Here 59

On the Winds of Canticle Wings, Awakened In Love's Soft Whispers Calling Home 61

Fly Free, Free of the Wingless Mold 63

The Authentic Ones Alive As Titillating Tenderness 65

Flourish As the Glory Sky of Infinity's Nurture Shine 67

Held As the Fresh Moment 69

The Eloquence-Happiness Is Sounding the True Clear Symphony of the Heart 71

The Unknowing Know Love, the Egoless Way Is Beauty 73

Warm Light Dawns in the Lillies of Forgiveness 75

Supple Grace Makes a Brilliant Opal Ivory Palace to Live In 77

Be The Kindness Nurture, the Springtime Warmth In the Midst of Every Blizzard of Gray 79

Clean Flourish Stillness Followed By Direct Selfless Action 81

Love Waits, Love Is, Ready In Celebration of Welcoming 83

The Peace of Infinite Tender Cradling 85

Softly Be, Gentle Celebration Inside, The Kind Hallelujah Unifies Inner and Outer as One 87

Unified Orchestras of Beauty Guard the Door of Consciousness 89

Faithful Here In Every Instant, Faith Is Trust Exonerated 91

Kindness Inside Is The True Refreshing Vitalness 93

The Beauty and the Weed; Every Concretized Limit Has a Path of Skyward Freedom 95

Mary Come to Us 97

Make a Symphony in the Dark Night, Sing Your Song 99

Eden's Rich Life, Heaven as Earth, Light as Formation, I Create by Being and Beholding 101

Incandescent Flourish, Grace Is the Revelation of Self-Completion by Infinite Giving 103

You Are Not Alone, I Care 105

Elegance Emerges Out of Opalescent Spaciousness, Rest in Unconditional Peace 107

Rest Abide in the Center White Space of Peace 109

The Reverent Resolute Ones, Warm the Wisdom Principle With the Sun of Love 111

Ecstatic Courage, I Am Here Forever 113

We Love, We Dance in the Shelter of Our Tender Thriving 115

Presence as Self-Kindness Shelters You in Trust's Violet Tender Vibrance 117

I Always Accepted You, Sacredness Accepted 119

Nurture Innocence, Courageous Glory, My Face an Ivory-Splendor Prayer of New Life 121

Indwell The Highest Mysteries of Love, Unspoken, Silent, Unseen 123

The Answer Is in the Soft On the Spot Response of Instantaneous Goodness 125

Stillness Emits Vibrant Caring and Bold Creative Beauty 127

True Opulence, Empty all the Way Down to Delicate Sheen Presence 129

Feel The Soft Celestial Smile of Faithfulness, That Resounds Silence 131

Easter Circle of Beginnings, Still Beginingless Presence 133

Ancient Oaks New Blooms, Every Season Our Love Endures-Shines in Calm Anointed Joy 135

Starburst Light Through the Ebony Path 137

Love Protects by Only Seeing the Pureness 139

Wisdom Clarity Here, Simple Noble Action Now 141

Still Sacred, Still Opulence As Givingness 143

Marry The Wonderment 145

The Formless Now Forms as the Answer (the Crystalline Foundation of Light Sustains the Blossom) 147

Love Origins Consciousness, Consciousness Knowing Itself, Where Form Appears 149

Before Thought Love Is, Tangible Rhythms of Light, Revealing Nascent Togetherness 151

Remember 153

Together Forever 155

Prelude
And Letter to the Reader

Dear Friend,

Welcome to this collection of sacred floral beauty, with inspiring contemplative titles.

Flowers reveal the exquisite and intricate beauty of creation. Each petal, each fragrance, speaks of heaven as earth, the celestial wedded to the tangible.

As original flowers of the Original God Presence, each individual being is a pristine, priceless emanation of the Essence-Presence of Eternal Beauty.

This *Eternal Beauty as God Presence* arises as *Deific Love,* as the Creator God giving Itself as Us, and we Give Ourselves as Love, as a universe of instantaneous paradise.

Seeing the beauty in nature, feeling the connection with flourishing Life, sparks remembrance of our Eternal Nature — endless aliveness as happiness, wonderment, and peace.

Before awakening to the full aliveness with/as God Presence, we all share a common existential pain — the grief of feeling separate from Love, from Creator, from our Original Opulence-Beauty Essence.

Everyone I have ever encountered to date, has at one time or another felt "not beautiful," not significant as a being, as Presence.

Very few beings have experienced themselves as truly *beautiful, beautiful, beautiful ... within ...as one with God Presence, a universe of limitless love and beauty in every instant ... as the reality and ground of being.*

Yet, in Beginning, in the Original peace void of the Original Night, from which the Mother God vessel originated us as *Living Light* —- we emerged-instanced as Deific Love, as the Light of Consciousness, as *Mother Father God Presence, as Original Light..... as Eternal Beauty upon Beauty upon Beauty.*

Your undeniable, eternal Origin and Essence is Eternal Beauty
So Beautiful as You
Eternal Beauty: You
Eternal Love: You

Serendipitously, at the time of creating this book, *So Beautiful As You,* the title song for the Mother Ahavah album simultaneously being recorded, sounded with this very phrase. The canticle song, *You Hold Me,* begins with:

I have never, ever seen
Anything So Beautiful
As You....

This reflects the wonderment of our adoration-love of our Creator and our Creator's love gaze of

beholding us as Eternal Beauty.

As you enjoy and engage with the flowers and arrangements in this book, reflect on the exquisiteness of your beauty. And feel this beauty of Self as you reflect upon this beauty essence of all flowers, all plants, all of the planet, all animals….all persons, all beings.

We exist as formless beauty and this Deific Love knowing Itself, this Light of Consciousness knowing Itself, evidences visibly, tangibly, as-in-beyond this formation of beauty.

May this book bless you with warm hearted moments that support you in feeling Home in the Heart

And may this book bless you with illuminative inspirations that serve you with guiding stars on your pathway of life.

Beauty Is….
So Beautiful as You
There is Nothing so Beautiful As You

You...

As the Eternal Love Glorious Life

You...

As unique individualization

As expression of simple peace And one-of-a-kind brilliance

You...

As an irreplaceable melodic note

A unique voice of expression In the symphony of the Whole

The sound bouquet of the Infinite

You...

Meeting the shadowlands

Of silver lined challenges

Dancing upon the pain of the aeons

And offering it all

To the perfect imperfections

Of the centerpointe of vulnerability

The gorgeous sheen of tenderness
You... Perfect As You Are

You... Perfect Love Origined as Eternal Beauty

Warm Blessings for Happiness, & Beauty

From My Heart,
Mother Ahavah
Home in the Heart Foundation

The Sacred Work of Dr. Ann Marie Nielsen

So Beautiful As You

70 Floral Creations

Love

Loves

For No Reason

Paradise

Be the Beauty Essence

Of the Changeless-Afresh

Pure Land

Inside...

Everywhere

Fall in Love

With

Love Knowing Itself

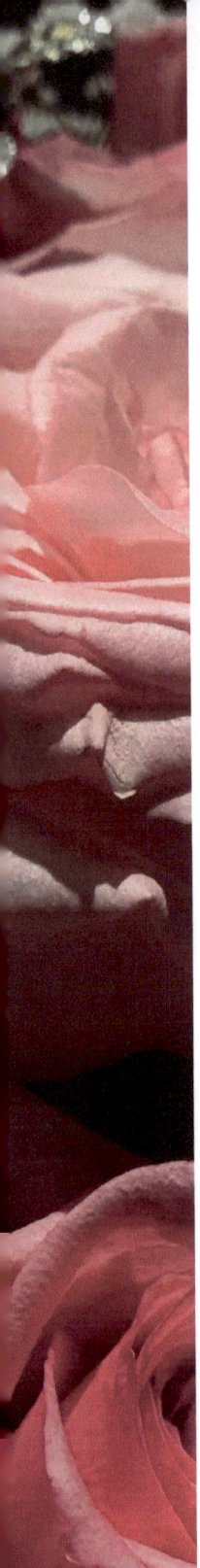

Hallelujah

Peace

Celestial

Sovereign

Awareness

Authentic Genius

Cradles Incandescent Innocence

In Bold Realness

I Am

The Silence

Of Love's

Tender Exalting

Crescendo

Soft

Is

True

The Prolific Heart

The Garden

Of Spontaneous

Joy-Nurture

At Home

I

Am

Here

For

Life

Simple

Bald

Vulnerability

Endures

In Eternal

Clean

Welcome

Tangible

White

Knowing

Seamless Holy Intimacy

Knowing Itself

Everyone Smiles Now

Before time

Ivory White Silence

Birthed My Essence

As *Original Stillness*

Bless Each Moment

See Gentle Peace Dawn

Delicate Goodness Power

On-the-Spot

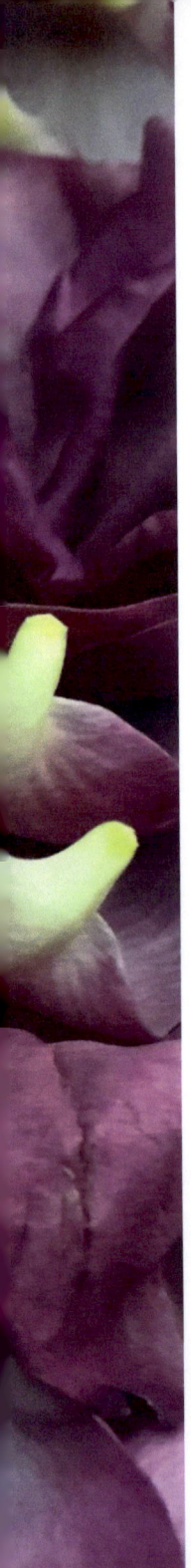

Cocoon

The

Potent

Focus

Compassion

is the

Priestess

of the

Prolific Industriousness

Delicate Freedom

Fresh to Bond

In each Moment

Jubilant

In Unified Non-Attachment

Reverence

Flourishes

The Moment

Instantaneity

Tomorrow's

Promise

Happens Now

Joy

Is Opening

To Be Deeply Touched

A Once Hard Place

Glows as

Soft Grace

Vulnerability is Strength

When we Rest

As the Sheen of *Acceptance*

Between the Two

That Makes not Two

Love

Finds

Safe Passageway

Here

On the Winds

Of Canticle Wings

Awakened

In Love's Soft Whispers

Calling Home

Embraced in Infinity

Home

Fly Free

Free of

The Wingless Mold

Your every Intricate

Ray of Brilliance

Offers Nascent Welcoming

In *Eternal Beauty*

The Authentic Ones

Alive As

Titillating Tenderness

Inside

In Each Moment

Flourish

As The

Glory Sky

Of Infinity's

Nurture Shine

Held

As The

Fresh Moment

The Eloquence-Happiness

Is Sounding

The True Clear

Symphony of the Heart

Without thought

For how it sounds

To another ear

The Unknowing

Know Love

The Egoless Way

Is Beauty

Sensitivity

Is together Love

Aware of the Real

Warm Light Dawns

In the

Lilies of Forgiveness

Supple Grace

Makes a Royal-Kind

Ivory Palace

To Live In

Be the Kindness

Nurture the Springtime Warmth

In the Midst of Every Blizzard of Gray

And Feel the Crisp Clarity

of Pure Clean Expression

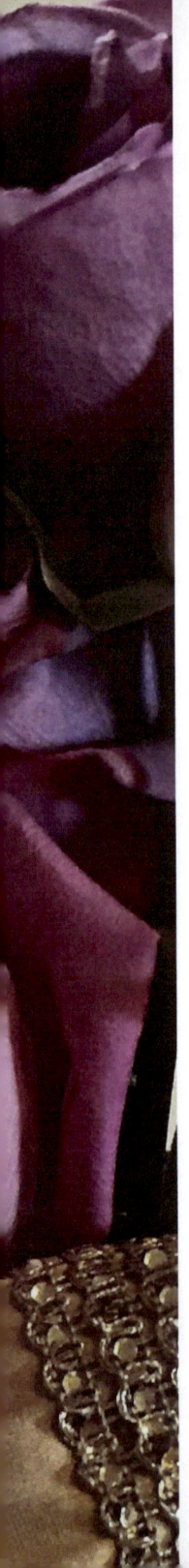

Clean Flourish

Stillness

Followed By

Direct Selfless Action

Without Commentary

Or Fanfare

Vivid Peace

Love Waits,

Love Is,

Ready

In Celebration of Welcoming

I Remember Us

Eden's Innocence

The Peace

of Infinite

Tender Cradling

Gentle

Victorious

Mastery

Illumines

The Way of the Heart

Softly Be

Gentle

Celebration

Inside

The Kind Hallelujah

Unifies Inner and Outer

As One

Unified Orchestras of Beauty

Guard the Door

Of Consciousness

Only Beauty

Enters Here

Only Beauty Is. . . .

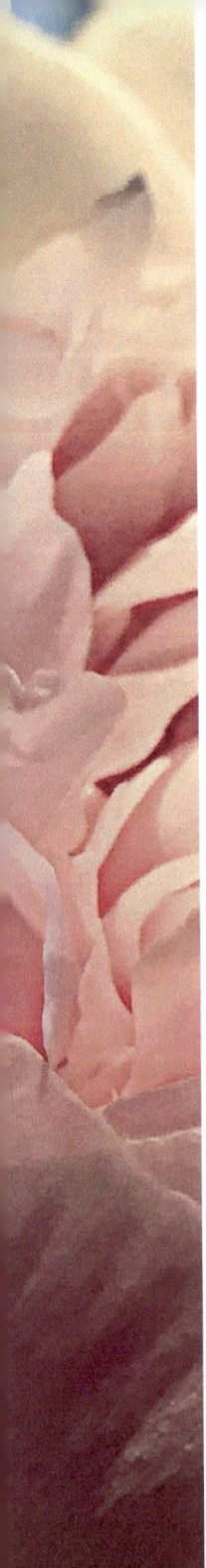

Faithful Here

In Every Instant

Faith Is

Trust Exonerated

Kindness

Inside

Is the

True Refreshing

Vitalness

The Beauty

And the Weed

Every Concretized Limit

Has a Path

Of Skyward Freedom

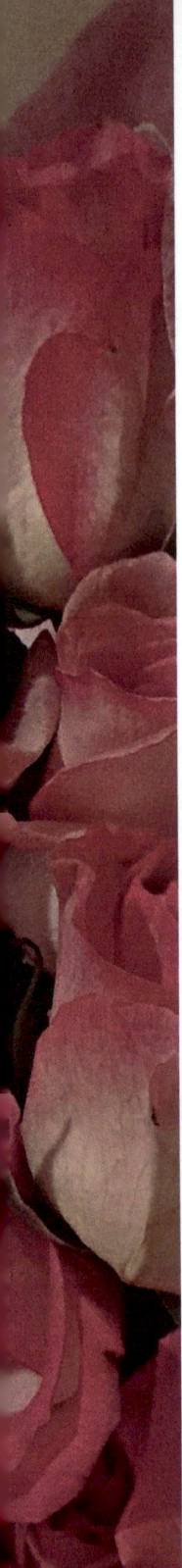

Mary

Come to Us

Make a Symphony

In The Dark Night

Sing Your Song

And In The Void

Your Song

Is The Garden of the Universe

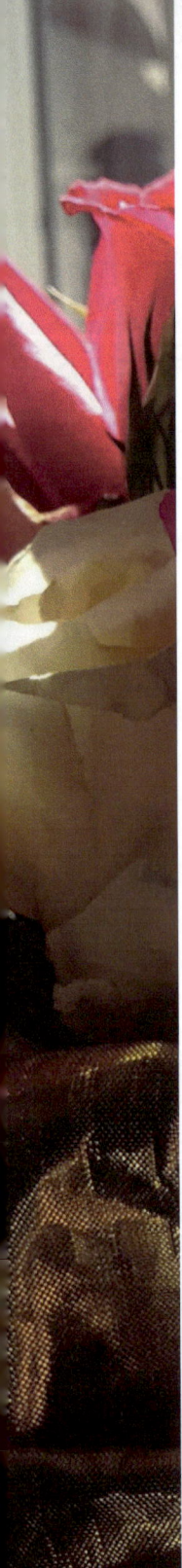

Eden's Rich Life

Heaven as Earth

Light as Formation

I Create

By Being

And Beholding

Beheld as Love. . . .

Incandescent Flourish

Grace Is

The Revelation

Of Self Completion

As Infinite Giving

You

Are Not

Alone

I

Care

Elegance

Emerges

Out of

Opalescent

Spaciousness

Rest in Unconditional Peace

Rest-Abide

In The

Center White Space

Of Peace

The Life Story

Rewrites, Re-Authors

In Shalom's Womb

Of Irresistible Fruition

The Reverent

Resolute Ones

Warm The Wisdom Principle

With The Sun of Love

To Brighten

Arising Inner-Outer

Landscapes

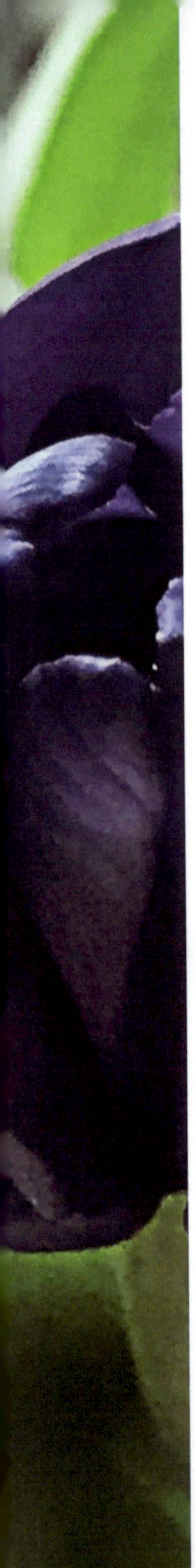

Ecstatic Courage

I Am Here

Forever

We Love

We Dance

In The Shelter

Of Our Tender Thriving

Presence

As Self-Kindness

Shelters You

In Trust's

Violet Tender Vibrance

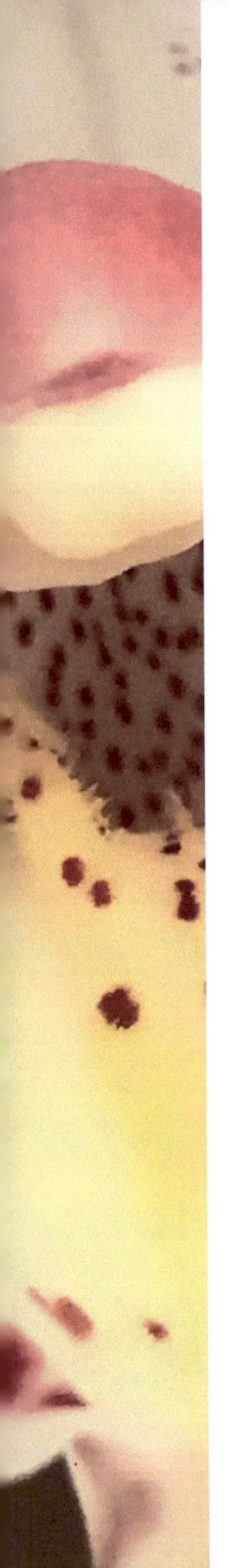

I

Always

Accepted

You

Sacredness

Accepted

Nurture Innocence

Courageous Glory

My Face An Ivory-Splendor

Prayer of New Life

Indwell

The Highest Mysteries

Of Love

Unspoken

Silent

Unseen

Yet, Being

The Pure Light

Carrying The Universe

The Answer

Is In

The Soft

On The Spot

Response

Of Instantaneous Goodness

Stillness

Emits Vibrant Caring

And Bold Creative Beauty

True Opulence

Empty All The Way Down

To Translucent

Delicate Sheen Presence

Aware of

Sheen Presence

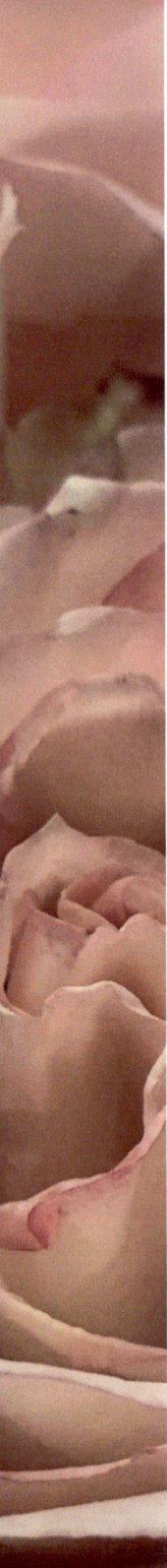

Feel

The Soft Celestial

Smile of Faithfulness

That Resounds Silence

That Blossoms

Unica Mystica Joy

Forever

Easter Circle

Of Beginnings

Still Beginingless Presence

Beholding Beginnings

as Hallmarks

Of the *Already Finished*

Completion

Ancient Oaks

New Blooms

Every Season

Our Love Endures-Shines

In Calm

Anointed

Joy

Starburst Light

Through The Ebony Path

Love Protects

By Only Seeing

The Pureness

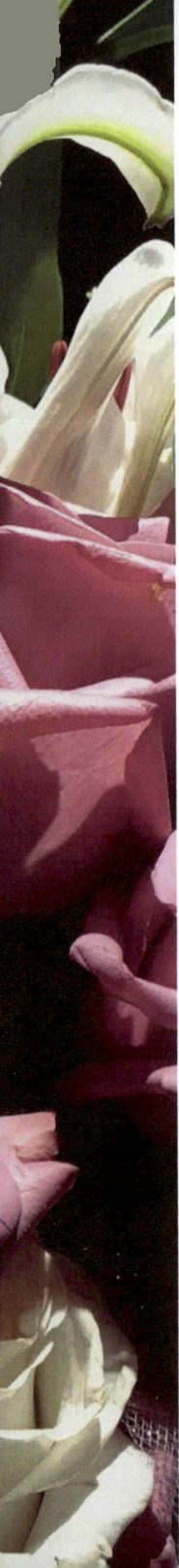

Wisdom

Clarity

Here

Simple

Noble

Action

Now

Still

Sacred

Still Opulence

As Givingness

Marry

The

Wonderment

The *Formless*

Now Forms

As The *Answer*

The Crystalline

Foundation of Light

Sustains the Blossom

Love

Origins

Consciousness

Consciousness

Knowing

Itself

Where Form Appears

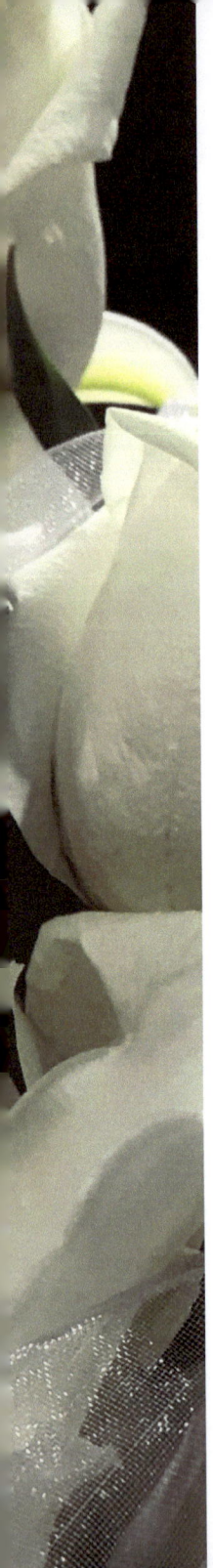

Before Thought

Love Is

Tangible Rhythms of Light

Revealing

Nascent Togetherness

Remember. . . .

Together

Forever

Holy Mother Carry Us

Emperor-Empress

Divine Mother Primal & Practical

Monolith Tower of Supreme Sensitivity

Shangri-La

Heaven

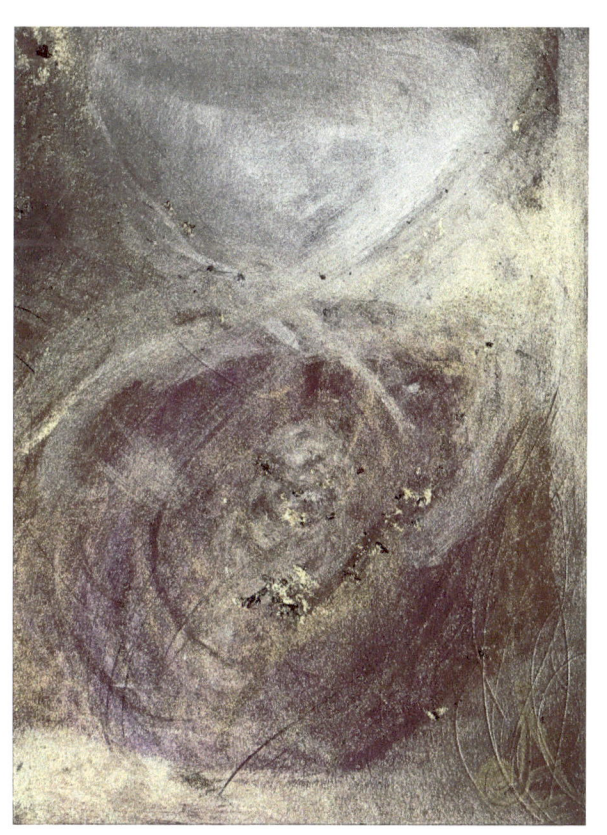

Other Books by Mother Ahavah

Diamonds of the Holy Heart

Pearls of the Presence

Holy Mother Carry Us

Father Ahavah

The Christmas Basilica

Paintings

Paintings selected from the Mother Ahavah Contemplative Awakening Art Gallery

You Hold Me — the Canticle album
from Mother Ahavah (Dr. Ann Marie Nielsen)

Ranging all the way from soft acappella tones, to epic instrumental orchestration with four part cathedral harmonies, this ascendant way of merging voice, tone and melody, offers you a deeply moving and elevating heart experience.

The Canticle songs immerse you in the felt remembrance of sacredness, peace, and Eternal Love in a way that liberation's awareness remains with you.

The Canticles originated as spontaneous songs of worship that Mother Ahavah, Dr. Nielsen sang and toned through the course her day — whether nestled in her prayer room, contemplating beneath the grandmother oak trees by the water, holding a retreat gathering, performing ministry activities of her Home in the Heart Foundation.

She had no plan to professionally record and distribute these tonings of stillness and grace—initially seen as offering silent blessings to the world in quiet moments, secretly and sacredly sang to heal and awaken hearts throughout our humankind family. In the recorded audios, Mother Ahavah sings the lead vocals, background vocals, four part harmonies and she tap dances the percussion.

Mother Ahavah, *You Hold Me* album

In the words of Mother Ahavah, "I clearly remember an intuitive flash as a child, that sound would one day emerge as a primary and powerful way to feel God's Presence. I had no idea at that time or until quite recently, that sound and song would arise as such an intimate and sacred expression of my voice in the world."

"The ineffable joy and love of God Presence, Face to Face is indescribable. I feel this experience pulsing through as melody and tones, which I usually initially tone without words for some time. Then spontaneously one day, lyrics arise. I entrust the hearing of these songs to you, that you rest in the Glory of our Creator, the beauty of your sacred heart."

Free samples of *You Hold Me* can be heard, and the album can be purchased at—

motherahavah.com/motherahavahcanticles.html

motherahavah.com

www.ingramcontent.com/pod-product-compliance
Lightning Source LLC
Chambersburg PA
CBHW041541220426
43664CB00002B/17